Revise THE NATIONAL TESTS

MATHS KEY STAGE 3

Bob Hartman
Eddie Wilde

Contents

The tests

The Key Stage 3 National Tests (SATs) are taken by secondary school students in May of Year 9. There are various tiers of entry, each of which is matched to the ability of individual students who will take all the papers at the appropriate tier.

The tests themselves are administered under exam conditions and are externally marked. Once marked, the papers are returned to school with the marks awarded and the overall level achieved (usually by the end of the Summer Term).

Revision

When revising, most successful students prepare, and stick to, a revision timetable starting several weeks before the tests. They choose specific topics at any one time and revise only these, making sure that the mathematics involved is fully understood. It is not a good idea to try and do all the revision in a short space of time or in one go. It is more effective to spend three half-hour periods working, rather than a solid two hours.

You will be expected to know certain formulas. Make a list and get a friend, parent, brother or sister to give you a quick test on some of them (it only takes about five minutes).

Using this book

The materials in this book are grouped by topic. There is a brief resumé of facts or methods that ought to be known, followed by an example question complete with the answer. It is a good idea to try working through the example question, looking at the answer to check that the topic is understood or to gain help where this is necessary.

There are Quick Questions for further practice where necessary and answers are provided later in the book. A small number of the questions on any given topic may be unfamiliar (e.g. only more able students will have been taught level 7 topics) but the other questions on the same topic will be appropriate. There is also an Extended Question which covers a range of different levels.

Doing the tests

Make sure you have a sharp pencil – when you have to plot points or draw lines or graphs you must do so accurately and blunt pencils will not allow you to do this.

Make sure you know how to use your calculator properly (e.g. how do the bracket keys work?, how do you clear the memory?, etc).

When you have to explain how or why something is so, try to use mathematical words in your explanation.

Do you want some extra marks (free!)?

The difference between being awarded one level and the next on the tests can be as little as one mark and simple mistakes often stop you doing well, so here are few basic tips each designed to help you get an extra mark:

1   Where the question tells you what units to use (most will) make sure your answer is in those units, e.g. if the answer should be in cm make sure yours is not in mm.

2   If the question asks for an answer to a number of decimal places, make sure you give just that. The same applies if a number of significant figures is asked for.

3   When answering questions on probability always give your answer as a fraction, decimal or percentage – nothing else is acceptable.

4   When solving an equation substitute your answer into the original equation to check that the answer you have really is correct.

What you need to know

A **fraction** has two parts: $\dfrac{\text{numerator}}{\text{denominator}}$. **Equivalent fractions** have the same value but different denominators and numerators.

The fractions $\dfrac{2}{3}$, $\dfrac{4}{6}$, $\dfrac{6}{9}$, $\dfrac{8}{12}$ and $\dfrac{20}{30}$ all have the same value, but $\dfrac{2}{3}$ is the **simplest form**.

Multiplying the numerator and denominator by the same number makes an equivalent fraction. Similarly, dividing the numerator and denominator by the same number also makes an equivalent fraction – this is sometimes called **cancelling**.

To change a fraction into a decimal, divide the numerator by the denominator, so to write $\dfrac{3}{32}$ as a decimal work out $3 \div 32$, which is 0.09375.

Examples

(a) Copy and complete these equivalent fractions:

   (i) $\dfrac{3}{32} = \dfrac{}{64} = \dfrac{21}{} = \dfrac{30}{}$ **(ii)** $\dfrac{7}{10} = \dfrac{}{20} = \dfrac{}{100} = \dfrac{28}{}$

(b) Write each of these in its simplest form:

   (i) $\dfrac{64}{132}$ **(ii)** $\dfrac{27}{117}$ **(iii)** $\dfrac{124}{372}$

(c) Change these fractions into decimals:

   (i) $\dfrac{5}{8}$ **(ii)** $\dfrac{5}{18}$ **(iii)** $\dfrac{5}{6}$

Answers

(a) (i) $\dfrac{3}{32} = \dfrac{6}{64} = \dfrac{21}{224} = \dfrac{30}{320}$ **(ii)** $\dfrac{7}{10} = \dfrac{14}{20} = \dfrac{70}{100} = \dfrac{28}{40}$

(b) (i) $\dfrac{64}{132} = \dfrac{16}{33}$ **(ii)** $\dfrac{27}{117} = \dfrac{3}{13}$ **(iii)** $\dfrac{124}{372} = \dfrac{1}{3}$

(c) (i) $\dfrac{5}{8} = 5 \div 8 = 0.625$

(ii) $\dfrac{5}{18} = 5 \div 18 = 0.27777777777...$

Decimals like this, which repeat, are called **recurring decimals**.

(iii) $\dfrac{5}{6} = 5 \div 6 = 0.83333333333...$ (also a recurring decimal).

Some recurring decimals have a long repeat pattern, for example:

$\dfrac{3}{7} = 3 \div 7 = 0.428571428571428...$

Examiner's tip

You usually need to write fractions in their lowest terms – but remember you can do this in 'easy' stages.

To find a fraction of something, for example $\dfrac{2}{5}$ of £45, first find $\dfrac{1}{5}$ by dividing by 5, which is $45 \div 5 = 9$. So, if $\dfrac{1}{5}$ of £45 is £9, $\dfrac{2}{5}$ will be $2 \times £9 = £18$.

Examples

(a) Find $\dfrac{5}{8}$ of 256   **(b)** Find $\dfrac{25}{100}$ of £300.

Answers

(a) $\dfrac{1}{8}$ of 256 is $256 \div 8 = 32$, so $\dfrac{5}{8}$ of 256 is 5 x 32 which is 160.

(b) $\dfrac{1}{100}$ of £300 is £3, so $\dfrac{25}{100}$ of £300 is 25 x £3 which is £75.

Quick Questions

1 Write these in their lowest terms:

   (a) $\dfrac{54}{126}$

   (b) $\dfrac{192}{320}$

   (c) $\dfrac{15}{100}$

   (d) $\dfrac{75}{100}$

2 Change these fractions into decimals, and say if any are recurring:

   (a) $\dfrac{12}{54}$

   (b) $\dfrac{16}{128}$

   (c) $\dfrac{6}{7}$

3 Calculate:

   (a) $\dfrac{1}{5}$ of 75 kg

   (b) $\dfrac{4}{5}$ of 75 kg

   (c) $\dfrac{3}{8}$ of 60 m

What you need to know

A quantity can be written as a fraction of another. This can be used to make comparisons. For example, in a test Jen got 12 out of 30 answers correct.

The fraction she got right was therefore $\dfrac{12}{30}$, which simplifies to $\dfrac{2}{5}$.

In a similar test, Rik managed 40 right out of 100, or $\dfrac{40}{100}$ correct,

which cancels down to $\dfrac{2}{5}$.

So both students did as well (or as badly) as each other. This was not obvious from their original test marks.

Examples

(a) What fraction is 32 of 256? Give your answer in simplest terms.

(b) Jan bought a packet of seeds containing 50 seeds.
He planted them all but only 20 of them grew.

   (i) What fraction grew?

   (ii) What fraction did not grow?

Answers

(a) $\dfrac{32}{256} = \dfrac{1}{8}$

(b) (i) $\dfrac{20}{50} = \dfrac{2}{5}$

   (ii) $\dfrac{30}{50} = \dfrac{3}{5}$

Percentages are another way of writing fractions which have a denominator of 100.

So 45% is another way of writing the fraction $\frac{45}{100}$ and $\frac{15}{100}$ is the same as 15%.

Using percentages makes comparisons easier.

Examples

Write these test scores as fractions and as percentages:
(a) 25 out 50
(b) 5 out of 20
(c) 7 out of ten

Answers

(a) $\frac{25}{50} = \frac{50}{100} = 50\%$

(b) $\frac{5}{20} = \frac{5 \times 5}{20 \times 5} = \frac{25}{100} = 25\%$

(c) $\frac{7}{10} = \frac{7 \times 10}{10 \times 10} = \frac{70}{100} = 70\%$

Quick Questions

4 In a full car park there are 75 red cars, 45 black cars, 30 white cars and 20 blue cars. What fraction of the cars in the car park are:
   (a) red?
   (b) black?
   (c) white or blue?

5 The average person sleeps for about 8 hours a day.
   What fraction is this of a whole day?

6 Write these percentages as fractions in their lowest terms:
   (a) 45%
   (b) 20%
   (c) 100%
   (d) 85%

7 In a survey, 4 out of 5 homes had a car. What is this as a percentage?

What you need to know

There is an easy way to find one **quantity as a percentage of another**:

* write the quantity as a fraction of the other

* change the fraction into a decimal

* then change this decimal into a percentage by multiplying by 100.

Examples

Write these test scores as fractions and as percentages:

(a) 45 out of 50

(b) 15 out of 75

(c) 9 out of 25

Answers

(a) 45 out of 50 is the same as $\dfrac{45}{50}$ $= 45 \div 50 = 0.9 = 90\%$ (0.9×100).

(b) 15 out of 75 is the same as $\dfrac{15}{75}$ $= 15 \div 75 = 0.2 = 20\%$ (0.2×100).

(c) 9 out of 25 is the same as $\dfrac{9}{25}$ $= 9 \div 25 = 0.36 = 36\%$ (0.36×100).

There are several ways of finding **percentages of quantities**.

Probably the easiest is to find 1% by dividing by 100 and then multiplying this by the number of per cent you want to calculate.

For example, to find 74% of 85, 85 ÷ 100 gives one-hundredth (which is 1%) = 0·85, and multiplying this by 74 will give 74%, which is 74 × 0·85 = 62.9.

Examples

(a) The population of a small town was 13 964. The population is expected to increase by 7%.
  (i) By how many is this?
  (ii) What is the new population expected to be?

(b) Calculate:
  (i) 43% of 168
  (ii) 100% of 643
  (iii) 150% of 600

Answers

(a) (i) 1% of 13 964 is 13964 ÷ 100 = 139.64, so 7% = 7 x 139.64 = 977.48 people.

  (ii) So the new population is 13964 + 977.48, which is 14 941.48 or about 14 941.

(b) (i) 1% of 168 is 1.68, 43% = 43 x 1.68 = 72.24

  (ii) 100% is one whole part ($\frac{100}{100}$) so the answer is 643.

  (iii) 1% is 6, so 150% is 150 x 6 = 900 or think of 150% as $\frac{150}{100}$ or 1·5, 1·5 x 600 = 900.

Quick Questions

8 In a bag of 25 potatoes 3 were bad. In another bag of 20 potatoes 2 were bad.
   Which of the bags had the larger percentage of bad potatoes?

9 Use percentages to decide which of these is the best performance:
   17 out of 50, 14 out of 40 or 9 out of 30.
   Which is the worst performance?

10 In a school of 1053 students, 97 were away.
   What percentage is this to the nearest 0.1%?

11 A cake weighs 1200 g, about 35% of which is flour.
   (a) What weight of the cake is flour?
   (b) What is the total weight of the other ingredients?

12 Here is the nutrient content of low-fat yoghurt.

Nutrient	% weight
water	86
fat	1
protein	5
carbohydrate	7
minerals	1

   Use these figures to calculate what weight of a 125 g portion of yoghurt is
   (a) water
   (b) protein
   (c) carbohydrate.

What you need to know

Brackets are used to group algebraic terms and numbers together, so twice the sum of 3 and 8 can be written $2 \times (3 + 8) = 2(3 + 8) = 2 \times 11 = 22$ and three times the sum of 2a and b can be written as:
$$3(2a + b) = 3 \times 2a + 3 \times b = 6a + 3b$$

Example

(a) Calculate the value of $5(12 - 8) + 2(4 + 3)$

(b) Simplify $3(5x + 6z)$

Answers

(a) $5(12 - 8) + 2(4 + 3) = (5 \times 4) + (2 \times 7) = 20 + 14 = 34$

(b) $3(5x + 6z) = 3 \times 5x + 3 \times 6z = 15x + 18z$

Examiner's tip

Any calculation put inside brackets is worked out first.
Brackets make the order of calculations clear. For example, $2 \times 3 + 1$ could mean 'two multiplied by three, then add one to the result', which is seven, or it could mean 'two multiplied by three add one', which is eight.
Using brackets the first one is $(2 \times 3) + 1 = 7$, and the second one $2(3 + 1) = 8$.

Example

Use a calculator to find the values of these:

(a) $(6.9 + 1.3) \times 1.5$

(b) $2.6(9.7 - 4.9) + 5.1$

(c) $\dfrac{34.3}{(2.9 + 5.1)}$

(d) $\sqrt{10} - \sqrt{6}$

Answers

(a) $8.2 \times 1.5 = 12.3$

(b) $= 2.6(4.8) + 5.1 = 17.58$

(c) $\dfrac{34.3}{(2.9 + 5.1)} = 34.3 \div 8 = 4.2875$

(d) $\sqrt{10} - \sqrt{6} = \sqrt{(10)} - \sqrt{(6)} = (3.162\ldots) - (2.449\ldots) = 0.71$ (2dp)

Simplify means to group together the same (or
like) terms, so x + x + x = 3x. Write as [number]
followed by [letter or letters].
The expression a + 2x simplified is a + 2x. You
can't combine a and 2x into a single term,
so a + 2x cannot be simplified further.

Example

Simplify these expressions

(a) x + x + x

(b) a + b + b + 2c − b

Answers

(a) 3x

(b) a + b + 2c

Quick Questions

1 Calculate the value of these:
   (a) $18 \div (2 + 4)$
   (b) $(43 - 8) \div 7$
   (c) $(22 + 29) \div (22 - 5)$
   (d) $15 \div (7 - 2)$

2 Simplify these:
   (a) $2(2x + y) + 3y$
   (b) $2(x + y + z) + 4(x + 2y)$

3 Put in brackets and + and − symbols
   to make these true.
   (a) 4   2   1   = 12
   (b) 5   6   1   5   = 30
   (c) 2   3   3   3   1   1   = 18
   (d) 5   1   3   6   3   = 53

4 Use your calculator to find these
   correct to 2 decimal places:
   (a) $\dfrac{7.84}{4.41 - 1.74}$

   (b) $2.3^2 + 1.7^2$

   (c) $\sqrt{8} + \sqrt{8}$

   (d) $8 - \sqrt{5}$

   (e) $49.3 \div (12.4 - 9.31)$

   (f) $\dfrac{26.4 + 1.26}{28.41 - 11.25}$

5 Simplify these expressions:
   (a) $2t + 6y + 4t$
   (b) $7a + 3a$
   (c) $c + c + c + 6c - 2c$

What you need to know

In algebra **substituting**, or **substitution**, involves replacing letters by numbers in an expression or formula. Here are a few rules used in writing algebraic expressions:

abc represents $a \times b \times c$, $a^2 = a \times a$ and $\dfrac{a}{c}$ represents $a \div c$.

Example

Find the value of the expression $6ab - a$, when $a = 2$ and $b = 3$.
When $a = 2$ and $b = 3$ the expression $6ab - a$ is $(6 \times 2 \times 3) - 3 = 36 - 3 = 33$.

When $x = 16$ and $y = 4$ find the value of:

(a) $\dfrac{2x}{y}$

(b) $\dfrac{x}{y^2}$

Answers

(a) $\dfrac{2 \times 16}{4} = 32 \div 4 = 8$

(b) $\dfrac{16}{4^2} = 16 \div 4^2 = 16 \div 16 = 1$

Examiner's tip

An expression like $6x^2$ represents $6 \times$ ('x squared').

When $x = 2$ this would be $6 \times 2^2 = 6 \times 4 = 24$ **not** '6×2' all squared.

Simplifying an expression means writing, for example, $4 \times b \times a \times 2c$, as $8abc$, we write the answer as the number followed by the letters in alphabetical order, which makes the answer easier to read.

Example

Simplify these expressions involving brackets:

(a) $4(a + b)$
(b) $a(a + b)$
(c) $2a(b + c)$
(d) $2a(a + b)$
(e) $2c(4c + 3d)$
(f) Simplify $2b \times 2a \times 2c$

Answers

(a) $4a + 4b$
(b) $a^2 + ab$
(c) $2ab + 2ac$
(d) $2a^2 + 2ab$
(e) $8c^2 + 6cd$
(f) $2b \times 2a \times 2c = 2 \times 2 \times 2 \times a \times b \times c = 8abc$

Quick Questions

6 When $a = 5$, $b = 2$, $c = 0$ and $d = 1$ find the values of these expressions
   (a) $ab + c$
   (b) a^2
   (c) $2a^2$
   (d) abc
   (e) $ab - cd$

7 When $x = 4$, $y = 8$ and $z = 2$ find the value of R in these formulas.
   (a) $R = xyz$
   (b) $R = \dfrac{xyz}{32}$
   (c) $R = 2x^2 - 4z$

8 Simplify these expressions:
   (a) $4c \times 8b$
   (b) $2x \times 10y$
   (c) $3x(2 + y)$
   (d) $4x(x + 2y)$
   (e) $3x(2x + 4y)$

What you need to know

Word formulas are ways of expressing formulas using words rather than letters, so, to change a speed in metres per second into a speed in miles per hour, you could use the word formula '*multiply by 11 and divide the answer by 5.*

Example

(a) A top sprinter can reach a speed of 10 metres per second.
What speed is this in miles per hour?

(b) Dragsters reach a speed of 100 metres per second.
What speed is this in miles per hour?

Answers

(a) $10 \times 11 = 110$ and $110 \div 5 = 22$ miles per hour.

(b) $100 \times 11 = 1100$ and $1100 \div 5 = 220$ miles per hour.

Examiner's tip

As usual, always check your working – read through the word formula again – and look at your answer and ask yourself if it looks sensible – 22 miles per hour seems OK for a sprinter but 220 or 2.2 miles per hour would not!

An **equation** is a true statement containing an equals sign, such as $2x + 1 = 15$. The value of x that makes the statement true is called the **solution** to the equation. You should always check your solution by substituting it back into the equation. If it is the correct solution, then both sides of the equation will be equal. We shall look at two ways to solve equations here. These are **balancing** and **trial and improvement**.

With **balancing** you treat both sides of the equation the same – so it will still balance. So for $x + 6 = 31$, subtracting 6 from both sides gives $x = 25$. The equation will balance if you: (i) add the same quantity to each side; (ii) subtract the same quantity from each side; (iii) multiply each side by the same quantity; (iv) divide each side by the same quantity.

With **trial and improvement** you try a solution; if the result is what you want, it is the correct solution. But if the result is not what you want, try another trial solution and so on.

So for $x + 6 = 31$, we are looking for a value of x such that $x + 6$ is equal to 31, for $x = 5$, $x + 6 = 11$ (too small), for $x = 30$, $x + 6 = 36$ (too large) and so on until $x = 25$.

Trial and improvement is used for more complicated equations than $x + 6 = 31$, for example, $x^2 + x = 25$.

Examples

(a) Solve these equations by balancing:
   (i) $2x + 8 = 60$
   (ii) $3a - 5 = 10$
   (iii) $5c + 5 = 4c + 21$

(b) Solve the equation $n^2 - n = 25$

Answers

(a) (i) $2x + 8 = 60$
      $2x = 60 - 8 = 52$ (-8 each side)
      $x = 26$ ($\div 2$ each side)
      Check if $x = 26$ is correct, then
      $(2 \times 26) + 8$ should be 60, which it is.

   (ii) $3a = 10 + 5 = 15$
      $a = 5$. Check $(3 \times 5) - 5 = 10$, which is the value of the right-hand side.

   (iii) $5c = 4c + 21 - 5 = 4c + 16$
      $5c - 4c = 16$
      $c = 16$.
      Check left-hand side
       $= (5 \times 16) + 5 = 85$;
      right-hand side
       $= (4 \times 16) + 21 = 64 + 21 = 85$,
      so LHS = RHS.

(Answer to (b) on page 16.)

Quick Questions

1 Your heart works very hard. It can be dangerous if it beats too quickly. Here is a rule for calculating a person's highest safe heartbeat rate. 'A person's highest safe heartbeat rate is their age in years subtracted from 220.'
   (a) A 40-year old goes for a jog. What is their highest safe heartbeat rate?
   (b) A 35-year old is exercising. Their heart beat rate is 200 beats a minute. Should they stop? Give a reason for your answer.

2 The higher you throw a ball, the longer it stays in the air. To find the height a ball reaches, in metres, use this formula. 'Square the time in seconds the ball stayed in the air, multiply this by 5 and divide the answer by 8.'
   (a) A ball stays in the air for a total of 4 seconds. How high did it go?
   (b) Pat managed to throw a cricket ball so that it stayed in the air for 13 seconds. She says it must have gone at least 100 metres up. Use the formula to see if Pat was right.

What you need to know

(b) trial value of n value of $n^2 - n$ .... (should be 25)

n	$n^2 - n$	
5	$25 - 5 = 20$	too small
6	$36 - 6 = 30$	too large
5.5	$30.25 - 5.5 = 24.75$	too small
5.6	$31.36 - 5.6 = 25.76$	too large

So we know the solution must be between $x = 5.5$ and $x = 5.6$

5.55	$30.8025 - 5.55 = 25.2525$	too large

So the solution must be slightly less than 5.55.
This means that to 1 decimal place the solution is $x = 5.5$.

Examiner's tip

Check your solution by substituting back into the original equation to make sure that LHS = RHS. With trial and improvement make sure your trials are getting better. It's a good idea to show all your working – just in case you make a slip, you may still get some method marks. The same holds for when you use balancing.

As well as solving equations, you may have to set them up or form them. Here are five steps that are useful to follow:

- Decide which quantity you need to find
  – check by reading the question through *at least twice*.

- Choose which letter to use to represent the quantity (or unknown) you want
  – don't forget to write down your choice, so its clear what you're doing.

- Use the information given in the question to make two expressions that are equal – these form either side of the equation.

- Solve your equation.

- Check that your solution fits the information you were given in the question
  – don't just check the equation, you may have set it up wrongly!

Examples

Form and solve the equations that fit these 'stories'.

(a) I think of a number double it, then add 9. The result is 29. What number was I thinking of?

(b) Amy's mother was 20 years old when Amy was born. Now she is twice as old as Amy. How old is Amy now?

(c) A rectangle is twice as wide as it is long. It has a perimeter of 36 metres. How long is it?

Answers

(a) Let n be the number, so $2n + 9 = 29$, giving $n = 10$, which fits the original story.

(b) Let x be Amy's age now, so her mother is now $2x$ years old, but Amy is 20 years younger than her mother so her mother is now $x + 20$ years old. We now have two expressions for Amy's mothers age which are obviously equal, so $2x = x + 20$, giving $x = 20$. If Amy is 20, her mother must be 40, and $2 \times 20 = 40$, so 20 must be right.

(c) Let c be the width of the rectangle, so its length is $2c$, but $c + 2c + c + 2c$, which is the perimeter, is 36 metres so $6c = 36$, and $c = 6$, giving the width as 6 metres and the length as 12 metres.

Quick Questions

3 Solve these equations:
  (a) $4n + 7 = 2n + 21$
  (b) $2c = 3$
  (c) $5x - 8 = 40 - x$

4 Solve this equation to 1 d.p.:
  $x^2 + 2x = 40$.
  The solution is between 4.5 and 6.5

5 The square root button on Liz's calculator has broken.
  Describe how she could find the square root of 90 to 1 d.p. by using trial and improvement.

6 Find and solve the equations that fit these 'stories':
  (a) 5 times a number take away 8 gives 13. What is the number?
  (b) When a certain number is multiplied by 6 and then 5 is added the answer is 47. What is the number?

7 The length of a piece of paper is 25 cm more than its width.
  The perimeter of the piece of paper is 450 cm.
  What is the length and width of the piece of paper?

What you need to know

The equals symbol '=' tells us that two expressions are equal, for example, $10 - 3 = 3 + 4$ or $2x + 1 = x + 7$. Expressions can be compared in other ways – an expression may be less than another. Symbols can be used to make statements comparing expressions like this.

Here are four of these **inequalities**.

$<$	**'less than'**	$12 - 3 < 5 + 6$	$2x < 6$
$>$	**'greater than'**	$12 \times 3 > 27 + 3$	$x + 5 > 12$
$\leq$	**'less than or equal to'**	$x \leq 10$ is true for $x = 10$, $x = 9.9$, $x = 5$, ...	
$\geq$	**'more than or equal to'**	$2x \geq 6$ is true for $x = 3$, $x = 3.5$, $x = 101$, ...	

Inequalities can be shown on a number line.

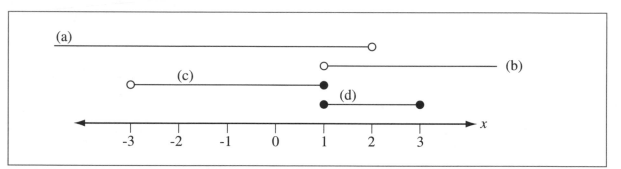

Line (a) can be described as $x < 2$, so possible values of x include 1, 0, -1.2, etc. but NOT 2.

Line (b) can be described as $x > 1$, so possible values of x include 2, 2.1, etc. but NOT 1.

Line (c) can be described as $-3 < x \leq 1$, so x may be -2.9 (but NOT -3), 0, 1, etc.

Line (d) can be described as $1 \leq x \leq 3$, so x can take any value from 1 up to 3.

Examples

(a) Write these as algebraic expressions involving inequalities:

(i) x has a value of at least 6
(ii) x is less than 5
(iii) x is greater than 2 and up to 10
(iv) x is less than, or equal to, twice y.

(b) Write down three possible whole number values of x for each of these inequalities:

(i) $x \geq 2$
(ii) $x \geq -2$
(iii) $2x > 10$
(iv) $x + 1 \geq 10$

Answers

(a) (i) $x \geq 6$
(ii) $x < 5$
(iii) $2 < x \leq 10$
(iv) $x < 2y$

(b) (i)   2, 3, 4, ...
(ii) $-2, -1, 0, 1, ...$
(iii) 6, 7, 8, ...
(iv) 9, 10, 11, ...

Examiner's tip

Always check that you have read the inequality the right way round. One way to do this is to substitute in a number and see if the result makes sense. Remember, for example, the difference between '<' and '≤'.

Quick Questions

8 Show each of these inequalities on a number line graph
   (a) $x \leq 0$
   (b) $x > 1$
   (c) $1 < x < 4$
   (d) $1 \leq x \leq 4$

9 Write these statements as algebraic inequalities:
   (a) The cost (C) will be between £100 and £200.
   (b) The journey time (T) will take more than 3 hours but less than 5 hours.
   (c) Your age (A) must be at least 18 in order to vote.
   (d) His test score (S) must be more than 70 to pass.

What you need to know

You should not use a calculator for any of this section.

You need to know your multiplication tables up to 10×10 by heart; to multiply and divide by 10, 100 , 1000, … and to do calculations like 20×4, 300×8 and $400 \div 50$ in your head. All these skills are needed to use **pencil and paper methods** to multiply and divide by 2-digit numbers.
Use methods that you feel most comfortable with.

Example

(a) Copy out and fill in the correct digits in these calculations:

   (i) $23 \times 17 = 20 \times \ldots\ldots + 3 \times \ldots\ldots = 340 + 51 = \ldots\ldots$
   (ii) $200 \div 40 = \ldots\ldots \div 4 = \ldots\ldots$
   (iii) $225 \div 15 = \ldots\ldots \div 3 = \ldots\ldots$
   (iv) $39 \times 64 = 40 \times 64 - \ldots\ldots = 2560 - \ldots\ldots = \ldots\ldots$
   (v) $128 \div 16 = \ldots\ldots \div 8 = \ldots\ldots \div 4 = \ldots\ldots$

(b) Use a pencil and paper method to calculate:
   (i) 63×79 **(ii)** 142×73 **(iii)** $164 \div 18$

Answers

(a) (i) $23 \times 17 = 20 \times 17 + 3 \times 17 = 340 + 51 = 391$
   (ii) $200 \div 40 = 20 \div 4 = 5$
   (iii) $225 \div 15 = 45 \div 3 = 15$
   (iv) $39 \times 64 = 40 \times 64 - 64 = 2560 - 64 = 2496$
   (v) $128 \div 16 = 64 \div 8 = 32 \div 4 = 8$

(b) Several different methods could have been used for these, only some are shown here:
   (i) $63 \times 79 = 63 \times 80 - 63 = 5040 - 63 = 4977$
   (ii) $142 \times 73 = 142 \times 70 + 142 \times 3 = 9940 + 426 = 10366$
   (iii) $162 \div 18 = 81 \div 9 = 9$

Examiner's tip

Use the method you know best. Always show your working when answering questions like these. If you have enough time, check your answer by using another method.

Estimating a calculation means looking at the calculation and replacing some or all of the numbers with ones that are easier to work with, so an approximate answer to $360 \div 48$ would be $350 \div 50$ which is 7 (the exact answer is 7.5). Estimating is not about guessing, it is about using numbers sensibly. Estimates can be used to check that an answer is reasonable – they can't show it's correct, only that it is probably wrong! To practise your estimation skills ask someone to set you some calculations – you estimate the answers – perhaps make a game of it. If you have time, it's always a good idea to estimate your answers – just as a check – try to get into the habit!

Example

(a) Estimate the answer to each of these. Show how you made your estimate.
   (i) 283×31 (ii) $63 \div 19$ (iii) $129.23 - 1.875$

(b) A parcel weighs 793 g. Does 9.57 kg seem about right for 31 of these parcels? Explain.

Answers

(a) (i) 283×31 is about 300×30 which is 9000
   (ii) $63 \div 19$ is about $60 \div 20$, so an answer of 3 would be reasonable.
   (iii) $129.23 - 1.875$ is roughly $130 - 2$ or round about 128.

(b) The calculation needed is 793×31 which is roughly $800 \times 30 = 24\,000$ g or 24 kg – the figure of 9.57 kg must be wrong.

Examiner's tip

Make sure you give a reason, if you are asked to explain your working or method.

Quick Questions

1 Calculate, using pencil and paper, the answers to these:
   (a) 214×92
   (b) $234 \div 13$
   (c) $555 \div 37$

2 An inch is approximately 25 mm. How many mm is:
   (a) 6 inches
   (b) 19 inches
   (c) 190 inches?
   How many inches is:
   (d) 425 mm
   (e) 5025 mm?

3 Estimate the answer to each of these. Show how you made your estimate.
   (a) 123×29
   (b) $122 \div 41$
   (c) 125×1.49

4 CDs cost £4.90. How many could you buy for:
   (a) £35
   (b) £48?
   Explain how you made your estimate.

5 A carton of cat food holds 48 tins. Felix eats a tin each day. Estimate how many cartons of cat food he needs in a year. Explain how you arrived at your answer and any approximations you made.

What you need to know

The **product** of 4 and 5 means 4×5, which is 20.
The product of 2, 4 and 5 is 40 ($2 \times 4 \times 5$).

Because 20 can be divided exactly by 4, we say 4 is a factor of 20.

A **prime number** has no other factors except itself and 1.

(1 is not prime, 2, 3, 5, 7, 11, 13, 17, 19, 23 are prime).

All whole numbers are either prime or made from the product of prime numbers, for example, $15 = 3 \times 5$ and $48 = 2 \times 2 \times 2 \times 2 \times 3$.

Any number that is an answer to the 6 times table is a multiple of 6 (6, 12, 18, … are all multiples of 6).
Because 4 is a factor of 20, this means that 20 is a multiple of 4.

Example

(a) **(i)** Write down all the factors of 12.
     (ii) Write down three multiples of 12.

(b) Here is a list of numbers:
    1   3   24 6   7   21   19
    Which of the numbers are:
    (i)   prime
    (ii) factors of 6
    (iii) multiples of 6
    (iv) have 2 and 3 as factors?

Answers

(a) **(i)** All the factors of 12 are: 1, 12, 4, 3, 6 and 2.
     (ii) Multiples of 12 are 12, 24, 36, …

(b) **(i)** 3, 7 and 19 are prime.
    (ii) 1, 3 and 6 are factors of 6.
    (iii) 6 and 24 are multiples of 6.
    (iv) 24 and 6 both have 2 and 3 as factors.

Make sure you don't muddle up 'factor' and 'multiple'. It's helpful to remember all the prime numbers less than 50.

Quick Questions

6   Jaki says that the expression
    $2n + 1$ generates prime numbers
    for $n = 1, 2, \ldots$
    Is she right?
    Explain your answer.

7   Duncan says that 'any number is
    either prime or is the sum of two
    primes'.
    Show that he is wrong.

8   Here are some statements. Rewrite
    them and insert the word 'factors' or
    'multiples' in the space in each
    case:
    (a) 4, 8 and 32 are all ....
         of 2.
    (b) 4 is one of the ....
         of 28 and 36.
    (c) 30 and 40 are both ....
         of 10.
    (d) 5 and 25 are both ....
         of 50.

What you need to know

The old Imperial units are still used, so you need to remember how to convert from some Imperial units to their metric equivalents:

- to change **miles** into **kilometres** multiply by 8 and divide by 5
  (for a very rough estimate multiply by 3 and divide by 2)
- to change **inches** into **millimetres** multiply by 25
- to change **pounds** into **kilograms** multiply by 9 and divide by 20
  (one pound is very nearly 450 g, and 1 ounce is roughly 25 g)
- to change **pints** into **litres** multiply by 3 and divide by 5
  (one pint is very close to 600 ml)
- to change **gallons** into **litres** multiply by 9 and divide by 2
  (one gallon is about $4\frac{1}{2}$ litres).

Example

(a) Here are some Imperial measures – change them into their approximate metric measures

   (i) 5 pounds (lbs)   **(ii)** 2 pints

   (iii) 3 ounces (oz)   **(iv)** 8 gallons

   (v) 12 inches

Answers

(a) **(i)** 5 pounds (lbs) is about 5 × 450 g which is 2250 g or 2.25 kg, or even 2 kg may be accurate enough.

   (ii) 2 pints is 2 × 600 ml = 1200 ml or 1.2 litres but, in some cases, 1 litre would be sufficient.

   (iii) 3 ounces (oz) is 3 × 25 = 75 grams.

   (iv) 8 gallons is 8 × 4.5 litres which is 36 litres.

   (v) 12 inches is 12 × 25 mm = 300 mm or 30 cm.

Examiner's tip

Always check that you have converted the 'right-way round': for example, 1 mile is greater than 1 km, so to change from miles to km you need to multiply by a number greater than 1. Similarly, one pint is less than 1 litre so the multiplier must be less than 1 in this case.

Measurements are never exact. When a length, for example, is given as 8 cm it does not usually mean it is 8.000000 cm long! It means that it is 8 cm to the nearest whole centimetre. This means it could be anywhere between 7.5 cm and 8.5 cm.

All these lines are 8 cm long to the nearest centimetre – check this by measuring.

If a ruler can measure to the nearest millimetre, which most short rulers can, a line given as 15 mm is between 14.5 mm and 15.5 mm long. So if a measurement is given as X, to the nearest unit, the limits of its possible values are half (0.5) of the unit less than X and half (0.5) of the unit more than X.

Example

(a) Write down the lengths of these lines to the nearest centimetre

(i)
(ii)
(iii)
(iv)

0 cm   1   2   3   4   5

(b) Which of these lengths are 2 cm to the nearest cm?   **(i)** 1.95 cm   **(ii)** 2.6 cm
(iii) 1.965 cm   **(iv)** 2.09 cm   **(v)** 2.51 cm

(c) For each of these measurements write down the range of possible values for the 'true' measurement: **(i)**   A mass of 21 kg
(ii) A temperature of 21°C   **(iii)** A bottle of volume 75 cl   **(iv)** A distance of 101 miles.

Answers

(a) (i)   1 cm   **(ii)**   4 cm   **(iii)** 4 cm   **(iv)** 4 cm
(b)   (i), (iii) and (iv)
(c) (i)   20.5 kg to 21.5 kg   **(ii)**   20.5°C to 21.5°C
(iii) 74.5 cl to 75.5 cl
(iv) 100.5 miles to 101.5 miles

Quick Questions

1 Here is part of the list of ingredients for making scones.
8 oz (ounces) flour
2 oz (ounces) butter
$\frac{1}{4}$ pint milk

Convert the measurements to approximate metric measures.

2 Change these records into their approximate metric measures.
   (a) Largest apple in the world weighed 3 pounds.
   (b) Largest spider in the world measured 11 inches across.
   (c) Deepest part of the Pacific Ocean is almost 7 miles deep.
   (d) Largest glass bottle ever made held 188 gallons.

3 Here are some measurements. For each one jot down the suitable units and a sensible degree of accuracy. For example, the length of this page would be in units of millimetres to the nearest millimetre.
   (a) Length of a playground.
   (b) Weight of a new-born baby.
   (c) Distance from Paris to London.
   (d) Height of a tower block.
   (e) Room temperature.

4 Which of these distances are 315 cm to the nearest centimetre?
   (a) 316 cm   **(b)** 3.15 m
   (c) 3151 mm   **(d)** 316.5 cm
   (e) 314.7 cm

25

What you need to know

Co-ordinates are a method of showing location using two numbers separated by a comma, e.g. (5, 3). In any pair of co-ordinates the **first** number is always the distance **across** and the **second** number the distance **up**.

Example

(5, 3) represents a point 5 units to the right of the origin (0, 0) and 3 units above it.

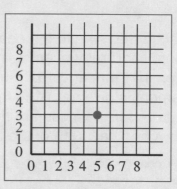

Examiner's tip

Pause to check that you are using co-ordinates the right way round – just in case!

You can use co-ordinates to plot **straight-line graphs**. The first number in the co-ordinate pair is the x value and the second number is the y value. You should plot a minimum of three pairs of co-ordinates to draw a straight line.

Example

To draw the line $y = 3x - 1$ first choose a sensible value for x (say 2). This would give a y value of 5, and the co-ordinates of the first point would be (2, 5). Do the same thing with different values of x (e.g. 1 to give (1, 2) and 3 to give (3, 8) to get two more co-ordinate pairs and plot all three points on a grid. Draw a straight line that passes through all three points. This is the line $y = 3x - 1$.

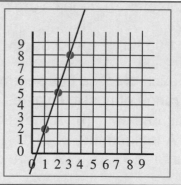

Examiner's tip

Check your straight line graphs by substituting in some values for x and y. Are they on the straight line?

To find the **equation of a straight line**
($y = mx + c$) you need the **gradient** (m) of the line
and also the **intercept** (c). To find the gradient you
need to work out the vertical difference divided by
horizontal difference. The intercept is the y-value of
the point where the line crosses the y-axis.

Example

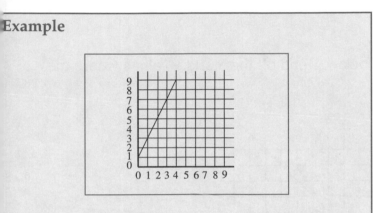

In the example above the vertical difference is 8
(the values rise from 1 to 9) and the horizontal
difference is 4 (the values rise from 0 to 4). This
gives a gradient of 2.

Answer

The line crosses the y-axis at 1, therefore the
intercept is 1. The equation of this line is therefore
$y = 2x + 1$.

Examiner's tip

Straight lines that slope down from left to right have
a negative gradient.

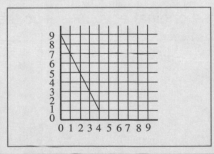

1   Write down the co-ordinates of the
    points marked on the grid.

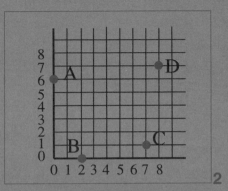

2   Draw a similar grid and mark on it
    these points: A(3, 6), B(0, 4),
    C(7, 2), D(6, 0) and E(4, 3).

3   Write down three pairs of co-
    ordinates that fit these equations:
    (a) $y = 2x + 1$
    (b) $y = 4x - 2$
    (c) $y = 3x + 2$
    (d) $y = 2x - 1$

4   Draw grids like the one in question 1
    and plot the lines in question 3.

5   Write down the equations of the lines
    on the diagram below.

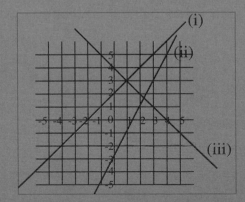

What you need to know

You can use graphs like these as one way to solve **simultaneous equations**. To do this you need to plot both of the given equations on a grid and read off the values of x and y where the lines cross.

Example

Solve the simultaneous equations:
$y = x + 2$ and
$y = -2x + 5$.

Plot the lines on a grid like the one below. Read off the x and y values where the lines cross to find the solution.

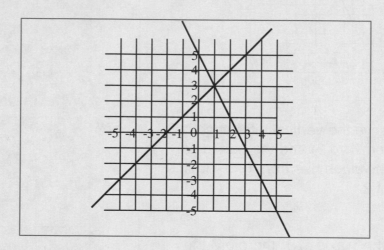

Answer

The solution to this pair of simultaneous equations is $x = 1$ and $y = 3$.

Examiner's tip

Check your solutions by substituting back into the original equations – do they fit?

Example

Solve the simultaneous equations

$$x + y = 7$$
and $\quad x - y = 3$

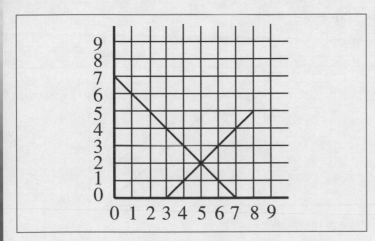

Answer

The solution to this pair of simultaneous equations
is $x = 5$ and $y = 2$.

Quick Questions

6 Draw a grid labelled from
$x = -5$ to $x = 5$ and
from $y = -5$ to $y = 5$.
Use straight-line graphs to solve
these simultaneous equations:
(a) $y = x + 1 \qquad y = 2x - 1$
(b) $y = x - 3 \qquad y = -x - 1$

7 Draw a grid labelled from
$x = 0$ to $x = 5$ and
from $y = 0$ to $y = 5$.
Use straight-line graphs to solve the
simultaneous equations
$$x + y = 4$$
and $\qquad y - x = 2$

What you need to know

The **sum of the internal angles of a polygon** can be found using this formula:

Sum = (2n − 4) × 90°, where *n* is the number of sides in the polygon.

Examples

(a) What is the sum of the internal angles in a hexagon?
Number of sides is 6.

(b) Four of the angles of a pentagon are 130°, 106°, 72° and 63°.
Work out the size of the fifth angle.

Answers

(a) Sum = [(2 × 6) − 4] × 90°   = 720°

(b) Number of sides is 5.
Sum = [(2 × 5) − 4] × 90° S   = 540°.
Missing angle   = 540 − sum of known angles
                = 540 − (130 + 106 + 72 + 63)
                = 540 − 371
                = 169°

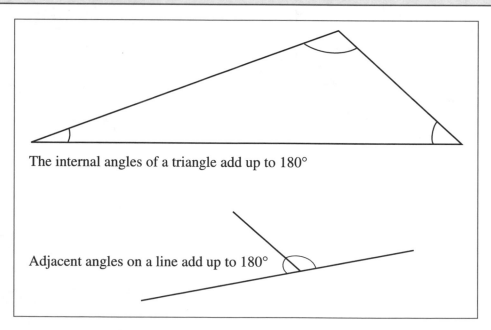

The internal angles of a triangle add up to 180°

Adjacent angles on a line add up to 180°

Example

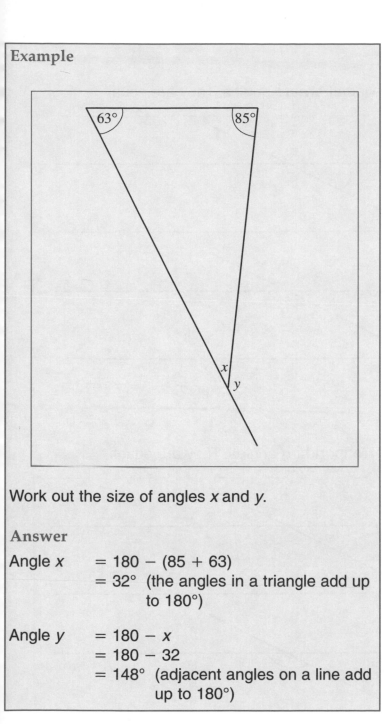

Work out the size of angles *x* and *y*.

Answer

Angle *x*   = 180 − (85 + 63)
            = 32°   (the angles in a triangle add up to 180°)

Angle *y*   = 180 − *x*
            = 180 − 32
            = 148°   (adjacent angles on a line add up to 180°)

Quick Questions

1   Work out the sum of the internal angles of an octagon.

2   Five of the internal angles of a hexagon are: 141°, 128°, 113°, 98° and 94°.
    Work out the size of the sixth angle.

3   Is it possible to construct a pentagon whose internal angles are 129°, 113°, 109°, 97° and 82°?
    Give a reason for your answer.

4   Four of the internal angles of a hexagon are 144°, 128°, 107° and 95°. The two remaining angles are both the same size.
    What is the size of each angle?

5   Work out the sizes of all the lettered angles in this diagram:

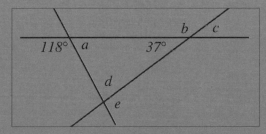

6   Explain why the information in this diagram must be wrong.

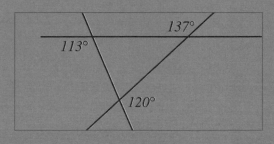

What you need to know

When dealing with parallel lines:

Angles such as the following are called **alternate** angles. They are equal.

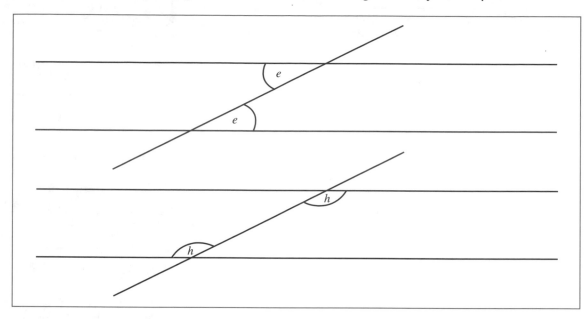

Angles such as these are called **corresponding** angles. They are equal.

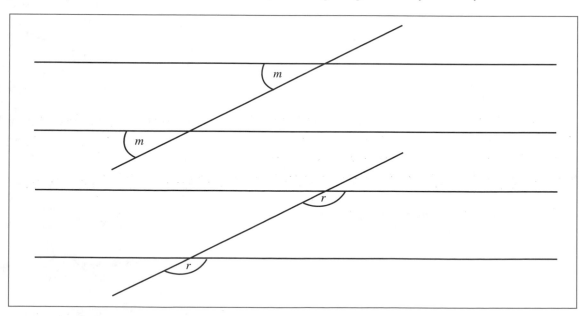

Angles such as these are called **vertically opposite** angles. They are equal.

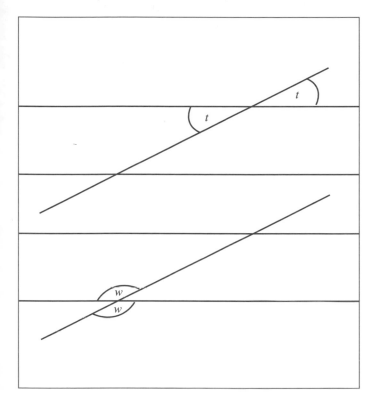

1 Work out the size of the lettered angles in each of these diagrams. Say which of the above facts you are using.

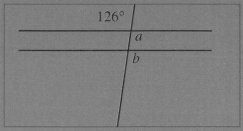

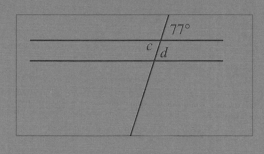

2 Use the information above to help you to work out the sizes of the lettered angles in this diagram.

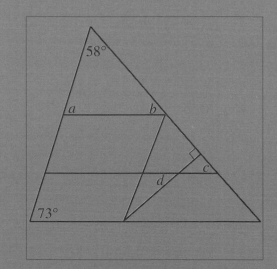

What you need to know

Shapes are **congruent** if their shape and their size are the same.

Shapes are **similar** if their shapes are the same but their sizes differ. With similar shapes one shape is always an **enlargement** of the other.

Example

These two shapes are similar. D corresponds to Z and C corresponds to Y.

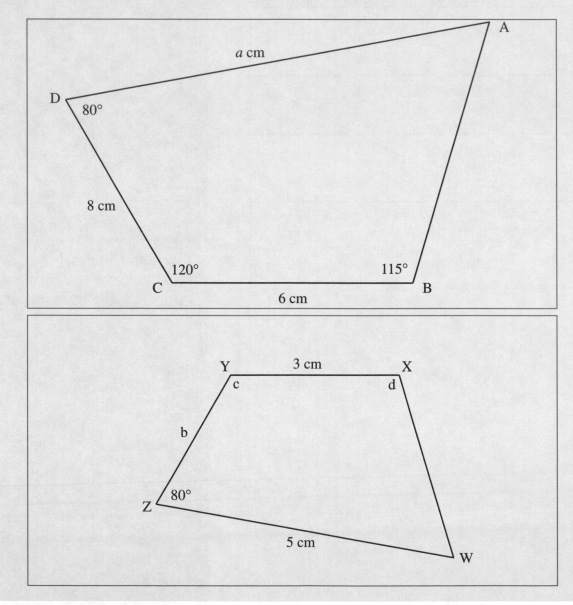

(a) Work out the length of sides *a* and *b*.
(b) Work out the sizes of angles *c* and *d*.

Notice that: Line BC corresponds to line XY and BC is twice the length of XY.
This tells us that ABCD is a two times enlargement of WXYZ. Therefore all the sides in the first diagram must be double the length of the sides in the second diagram.

Answers

(a) Side *a* is 10 cm and side *b* is 4 cm.
(b) Angle *c* is 120° and angle *d* is 115°.

Examiner's tip

When dealing with similarity/enlargement the angles never change size.

1 These shapes are not drawn to scale.
   (a) Which of these shapes are congruent?
   (b) Which of the shapes are similar?

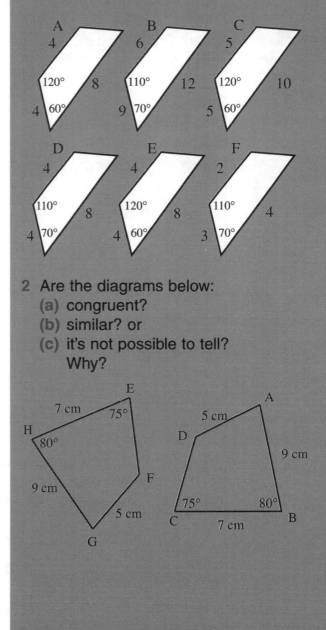

2 Are the diagrams below:
   (a) congruent?
   (b) similar? or
   (c) it's not possible to tell?
      Why?

What you need to know

You must learn these formulas:

The **area** of a circle can be found using the formula **Area** $= \pi r^2$ where r is the radius of the circle.

The **circumference** of a circle can be found using the formula **Circumference** $= \pi D$, where D is the diameter of the circle or **Circumference** $= 2\pi r$, where r is the radius of the circle.

Example

Tree plates are sometimes used in ornamental gardens to protect the root area around trees and as a decorative feature. One type is made in two identical pieces which are joined when placed around the tree.

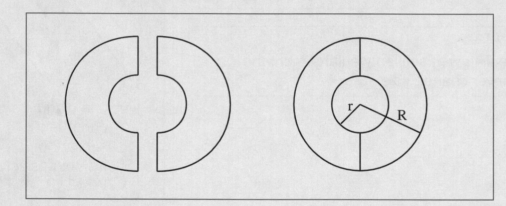

If the radius of the inner circle (r) is 25 cm and the radius of the outer circle R is 60 cm work out (take π to be 3.142):

(a) the area of the inner circle
(b) the circumference of the outer circle
(c) the total perimeter of one of the pieces.

Answers

(a) Area $= \pi r^2$
$= 3.142 \times 25^2$
$= 3.142 \times 625$
$= 1963.75 \, \text{cm}^2$

(b) Circumference $= \pi \times D$
$= 3.142 \times (2 \times 60)$ Diameter *not* radius
$= 3.142 \times 120$
$= 377.04 \, \text{cm}$

(c) Total perimeter of one piece =
half perimeter of large circle + half perimeter
of small circle + two straight edges.
Perimeter of large circle = 377.04 cm (see (b)
above)
half perimeter = 188.52 cm.

Perimeter of small circle = $\pi \times D$
= 3.142 × 50
= 157.10 cm
Half perimeter = 78.55 cm

Straight edge = $R - r$
= 60 − 25
= 35 cm
Two straight edges = 70 cm

Total perimeter of piece
= 188.52 + 78.55 + 70
= 337.07 cm

Examiner's tips

Make sure you learn the two formulas and don't get
radius and diameter muddled up – it's easy to do
this in a test – spend a few moments checking.
Also, remember that πr^2 means $\pi \times r \times r$ *not* $(\pi r)^2$
or $\pi \times r \times 2$.

It can be a big help to sketch the information given
in a problem, so that you can 'see' what's
happening a lot easier.

Quick Questions

1 (a) Work out the area of a circle
        with a diameter of 18 cm.
   (b) Work out the circumference of a
        circle with radius 12 cm.

2 The shape below has semicircular
   ends. Work out:
   (a) its area and
   (b) its perimeter.

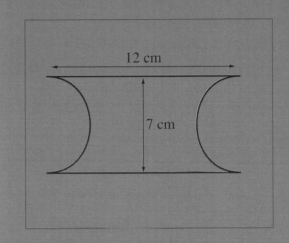

3 A practice running track is in the
   shape of a rectangle with two semi-
   circles on each of the shorter ends.
   The rectangular part measures 100
   metres by 50 metres. Work out the
   track's:
   (a) perimeter
   (b) area.

What you need to know

A **number sequence** is a list of numbers, called **terms**, which have a rule connecting them. Some sequences have names, for example,

Counting or **whole numbers**: 1, 2, 3, 4, 5, …
Odd numbers: 1, 3, 5, 7, 9, …
Even numbers: 2, 4, 6, 8, 10, …
Square numbers: 1, 4, 9, 16, 25, …
Triangle numbers: 1, 3, 6, 10, 15, …
Fibonacci numbers: 1, 1, 2, 3, 5, 8, 13, …

The symbol '**...**' means '*and so on in the same way*'.

Example

Describe these sequences:
(a) 10, 15, 20, 25, 30
(b) 24, 22, 20, 18, 16

Answers

(a) Multiples of 5.
(b) Reducing sequence of even numbers.

A number sequence may be described, in words or using algebra, by the pattern or rule that it follows. The rule for making (**generating**) a number sequence can sometimes involve the **position of a term**.

Example

Write down a rule to generate terms in these sequences:

(a)

Position	1	2	3	4
Term	4	11	18	25

(b)

Position	1	2	3	4
Term	45	39	33	27

(c) Write down, using algebra, the rule for the sequences above using position and term.

Answers

(a) You are adding on 7 each time.

(b) You are subtracting 6 each time.

(c) *T* represents term and *P* represents position.

For (a) $T = 7P - 3$

For (b) $T = 51 - 6P$

The important thing here is to use the term to term difference as a starting point. Multiply each position number by the difference and then see what adjustment needs to be made to generate the sequence.

For (a) 7 times position gives 7 14 21 28. To get the sequence you must take away 3 each time so the rule is $7 \times P - 3$ or $7P - 3$.

For (b) be careful! The difference here is -6. Multiplying the position number by -6 gives -6 -12 -18 -24.

To get the sequence you need to add on 51 each time so the rule is $-6 \times P + 51$ or $-6P + 51$ or $51 - 6P$.

Examiner's tip

Always check that your rule works for *all* the terms you have been given.

Quick Questions

1 Write down the next two numbers in these sequences:

   (a) 10, 13, 16, 19, 22,...

   (b) 16, 25, 36, 49, 64, ...

   (c) 12, 15, 18, 21, 24, ...

   (d) 2, 2, 4, 6, 10, 16, ...

2 Write down the position to term rule for these sequences:

(a)

Position (P)	1	2	3	4
Term (T)	9	13	17	21

(b)

Position (P)	1	2	3	4
Term (T)	22	19	16	13

What you need to know

Spotting a rule for a sequence may be helped by looking at the **differences** between terms.

Example

Write down the rule to generate terms in this sequence:

Position:	1	2	3	4	5
Term:	2	8	16	26	38

Answer

The numbers in this sequence go up by 6, then 8, then 10, then 12; this is not a constant amount each time and it is therefore not a simple sequence. You may have spotted that the amount that the sequence increases by does have a pattern of its own – they each go up by 2. This fact is useful in finding the rule.

Position:	1	2	3	4	5	
Term:	2	8	16	26	38	
1st difference		6	8	10	12	This is not constant.
2nd difference			2	2	2	This is constant and means that the rule we are looking for must involve a square.

The table below helps to find the rule.

Squares	1	4	9	16	25
Term	2	8	16	26	38
Term − Squares	1	4	7	10	13

The differences here are constant and the method for simple sequences gives a rule of $3x - 2$. When this is combined with the x^2 it gives an overall rule of $x^2 + 3x^2 - 2$ for the original sequence.

Algebra is a useful way to write down rules connecting numbers in a sequence.
Before using any algebra make a table of results – this will show up any patterns.

Example

The picture is of some Scissor Tongs used by a sheet metal worker to put rivets into panels. These are size 5 tongs because there are 5 sections to the tongs. There are 6 centre bolts, 10 pivot pins and 8 full arms in these tongs.

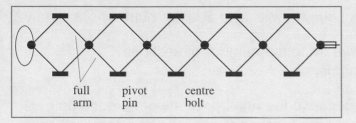

full arm   pivot pin   centre bolt

For any size of tong find:
(a) a rule linking the number of centre bolts to the number of sections
(b) a rule linking the number of pivot pins to the number of sections
(c) a rule linking the number of full arms to the number of sections.

(Answers on page 42.)

Examiner's tip

With questions like this it usually helps to draw a table of results – that way any patterns become clear.

Quick Questions

3 Write down the position to term rule for these sequences:
(a)

Position (P)	1	2	3	4	5
Term (T)	2	7	14	23	34

(b)

Position (P)	1	2	3	4	5
Term (T)	3	4	7	12	19

4 A large crane is erected by joining together a number of sections.
The sections are box shaped and have four identical sides. Each side looks like this and can be made in different lengths:

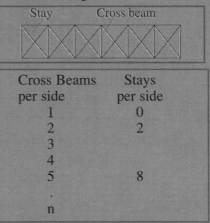

Cross Beams per side	Stays per side
1	0
2	2
3	
4	
5	8
.	
n	

(a) Complete the table above for the number of Cross Beams and Stays in one side.
(b) What is the formula linking the number of Stays (S) to the number of Cross Beams (C) in one side?
(c) Write down a formula linking the total number of Stays (S) to the total number of Cross Beams (C) in a section.

41

Sequences

What you need to know

Answers

Sections	Centre bolts	Pivot pins	Full arms
1	2	2	0
2	3	4	2
3	4	6	4
4	5	8	6
5	6	10	8

(a) The number of centre bolts is always 1 more than the number of sections.
The rule is centre bolts = sections + 1
or
$B = S + 1$ (where B is number of centre bolts and S is the number of sections)

(b) The number of pivot pins is always twice the number of sections
The rule is pivot pins = 2 × sections, or $P = 2S$.

(c) The rule is not as easy to spot. Because the number of full arms goes up by 2 each time, the rule must be 2 times the number of sections and some other adjustment:
Twice the number of sections gives us   2   4   6   8   10
but we want   0   2   4   6   8
The way to get these numbers is to subtract 2 from twice the number of sections.
The rule is:
full arms = (2 × Sections) − 2
or
$A = 2S − 2$ (where A is the number of arms). One way to check this is to notice that the number of full arms is always 2 less than the number of pivot pins. In other words full arms = pivot pins − 2.
Since we have a formula for pivot pins in part (b) we can substitute this into the formula above to get full arms = (2 × Sections) − 2
or
$A = 2S − 2$.

Quick Questions

5 A fence maker uses hexagonal panels as a basic pattern.

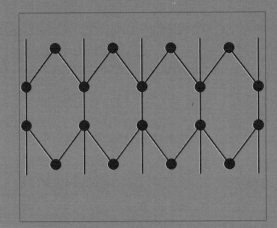

At every joint he places a steel rose. Draw a suitable table for fences up to 6 panels showing the number of panels, the number of posts and the number of roses used. Write down a formula linking the number of panels to the number of roses.

What you need to know

The **range** of a set of data is the difference between the highest and lowest values. For a given set of data there are three types of 'average':

Mean –   add all the data items together and divide the total by the number of data items.

Median –   when all data items are placed in order of size the median is the middle one.

Mode –   this is the most frequently occurring data item.

Example

The following are the ages of people entering a swimming pool one evening:

13	7	31	8	14	12	61	10	27
5	44	36	16	6	15	13	28	11
14	55	35	31	13	39	15	26	9

Work out:
(a) the mean   **(b)** the median
(c) the mode   **(d)** the range for this set of data.

Answers

(a) There are 27 data items and the total is 594. The mean is 22 (594 divided by 27).
(b) First, put all the ages in order.
   5 6 7 8 9 10 11 12 13 13 13 14 14 15 15 16 26 27 28 31 31 35 36 39 44 55 61
   Now find the middle one. The median is 15.
(c) Look at the list in part (b) and find
   the age that occurs most often.
   The mode is 13.
   Note: If more than one number occurs the most then you must write down each of them. For example, if the number 31 had also occurred
   three times the mode would have been 13 and 31.
(d) The highest value is 61 and the lowest 5. This gives a range of 56.

Examiner's tips

Always check to make sure you haven't muddled up mean, mode and median – it's easy to do in a test!

Remember range is the difference between the highest and lowest value, don't write the range as 4 to 10 which is wrong, it should be 6 (10 − 4).

Remember a result of 0 must be treated like any other result value – you can't just ignore it, so for the set of numbers: 0, 0, 0, 0, 10, the range is 10, mode is 0, median is 0 and mean is 2.

To compare two **distributions** (the arrangement of the values of each set of data) you must comment about the range of the data for each set and comment on either the mean, median or mode as appropriate.

Example

The children in a swimming club record the time it takes them to do one length of backstroke. The results are in the table below:

Boys   45 48 60 42 53 47 51 54 49 48 47 53
        48 44 46
Girls   45 47 55 46 53 63 48 50 46 51 48 48

Answers

Compare the distributions of times for boys and girls. There are 15 boys and their mean time is 49 seconds (735 ÷ 15). The range of their times is 18 seconds (60 − 42).
There are 12 girls and their mean time is 50 seconds (600 ÷ 12). The range of their times is also 18 seconds (63 − 45). The median and mode are both 48 for both groups. The mean time for the boys (49) is slightly faster than the girls' (50) but the range, mode and median are the same for both groups.

Quick Questions

1   When Jamie swims 50 m he records the time it takes. Here are the times (in seconds) that he records: 85 78 94 101 83 95 88 79 97 84.
    Work out the mean and range for this set of data.

2   The following is the number of 'conkers' collected from individual chestnut trees on one day in October:
    0   0   3   17   6   0   5   2   8
    12   1   5   6.
    Work out the mean, median and mode for this set of data.

3   Here are the times taken, in seconds, by two athletes to run 100 metres.

Jean:	11.8	11.4
11.0	11.4	11.8
11.2	11.4	11.2
11.4	11.4	
Sue:	12.0	11.8
11.0	11.8	11.6
11.8	11.2	

Compare the distribution of times for the two athletes.
Overall who do you think was the better 100 metres runner?
Give reasons for your choice.

What you need to know

Distributions may also be shown as **frequency diagrams** or **frequency tables**.
It is still possible to calculate the mean, mode, median and range by reading from the chart or table and calculating.

Example

Find the mean, mode, median and range for these two different mark distributions.

Frequency diagram

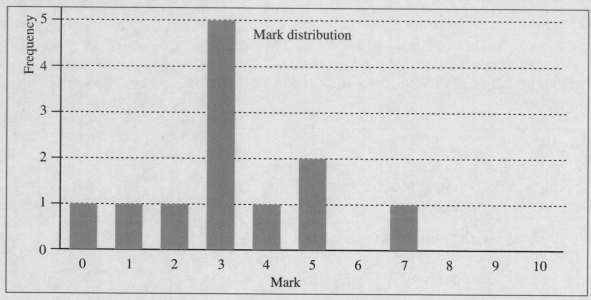

Frequency table

Mark	0	1	2	3	4	5	6	7	8	9	10
Frequency	1	1	2	5	2	1	0	0	0	0	0

For the data on the frequency diagram

By adding up the frequencies we can find the total number of results, which is
1 + 1 + 1 + 5 + 1 + 2 + 1 = 12.
The total number of marks scored by this group of 12 people is
$(0 \times 1) + (1 \times 1) + (2 \times 1) + (3 \times 5) + (4 \times 1) + (5 \times 2) + (6 \times 0) + (7 \times 1) = 39$.
So the mean mark is 39 ÷ 12 = 3.25.
Mode (or modal) mark is 3 (very easily read straight from the chart).
Median (or middle mark) is 3 (the mark between the 6th and 7th person in order, which can be read straight off the chart).
The range of marks is 7 − 0 which is 7 marks.

For the data in the frequency table

By adding up the frequencies we can find the total number of results, which is
1 + 1 + 2 + 5 + 2 + 1 = 12.
The total number of marks scored by this group of 12 people is $(0 \times 1) + (1 \times 1) + (2 \times 2) + (3 \times 5) + (4 \times 2) + (5 \times 1) + (6 \times 0) = 33$.
So the mean mark is $33 \div 12 = 2.75$.
The mode (or modal) mark is 3 (very easily read straight from table).
The median (or middle mark) is 3 (the mark between the 6th and 7th person in order, which can be read straight off the table).
The range of marks is $5 - 0$ which is 5 marks.

Examiner's tip

Check that the total of the frequencies gives the total number of items of data, including items that are zero, and check that, when finding the total, you add (frequency × value) for all the results, including the ones that have a value of zero.

Quick Questions

4 Find the number of students taking each of these tests and the mean, modal mark and range for each test.

Mark distribution A

mark	frequency
0	2
1	0
2	0
3	2
4	3
5	2
6	0
7	1
8	0
9	1
10	0

Mark distribution B

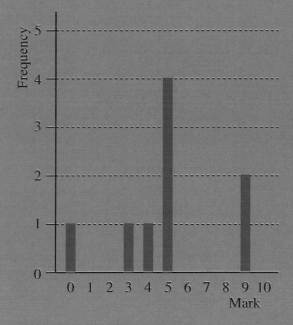

What you need to know

Pie charts are a useful way of showing information. They can be constructed using either **angles** (with an angle measurer or protractor) or **percentages** (with a pie chart scale).

Example

A grain merchant expects to sell the following number of sacks of grain:
Barley: 12 000   Corn: 15 000   Maize: 9 000   Wheat: 24 000

Draw a pie chart to show this information.

Answers

Work out the total number of sacks (60 000) and then the fraction that each grain type represents. Next multiply by either 100 to get a percentage or 360 to get degrees.

	Percentage	Degrees
Barley: 12 000/60 000	20	72
Corn: 15 000/60 000	25	90
Maize 9 000/60 000	15	54
Wheat: 24 000/60 000	40	144

Using your pie chart scale or angle measurer carefully construct the pie chart.

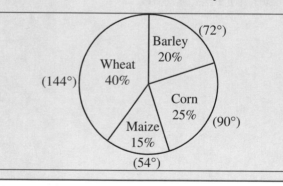

Examiner's tip

Always draw in pencil (a sharp one is best). Draw each line in turn and remember to measure the next sector from the line just drawn and not from the beginning each time.

Most pie charts in newspapers do not have the percentages shown on them. Not many people carry pie chart scales about with them either! So it is important to be able to estimate percentages from pie charts. It helps to have a picture of the 'easy' percentages like these.

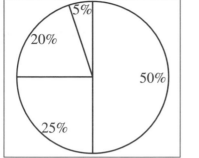

5 Josh collected the following data from his year about the type of lunch they preferred.

School meal (hot)	48
School meal (salad)	37
Packed lunch	43
Snack bar	56
Go home	12

Draw a pie chart to show this information.

6 This pie chart shows how Mike spends his day.

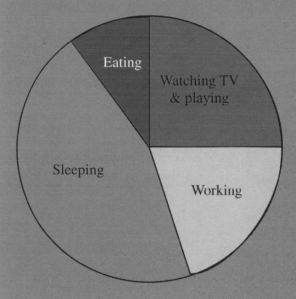

Estimate what percentage of his time Mike spent:
(a) watching TV and playing
(b) eating
(c) not watching TV and playing
(d) working.

Example

This pie chart shows the relative areas of the world's four oceans.

(a) About what fraction of the total ocean area is the Pacific?
(b) About what percentage is the Atlantic?
(c) About what percentage is the Arctic?

Answers

(a) About half the area is taken by the Pacific Ocean.
(b) About 25% of area is taken by the Atlantic Ocean.
(c) About 5% of area is taken by the Arctic Ocean.

Examiner's tip

Remember a half is 50%, a quarter is 25%, a third is roughly 30% and three quarters is 75%, also all the percentages should add up to 100% – a whole pie.

What you need to know

The **probability** of any event happening is expressed using a number ranging from 0 to 1 where 0 means it is **impossible** for the event to happen and 1 means the event is **certain** to happen.

The probability of any event happening is the number of acceptable **outcomes** (ways the event can happen) divided by the number of possible outcomes.

Example

There are 7 red, 5 green, 4 blue and 4 yellow balls in a bag.
One ball is pulled out without looking.
What is the probability that the ball is:
(a) green   (b) blue or red   (c) black?

Examiner's tip

Probabilities should be written as fractions or as decimals and not as odds.
Always make sure that your probabilities are between zero and one – you can't have a negative probability or one greater than 1!

Answers

(a) There are 5 green balls and 20 balls in total so the probability of picking a green ball is $\frac{5}{20}$ or $\frac{1}{4}$ or 0.25.

(b) The number of balls that are blue or red is 11 and there are 20 balls in total, so the probability of picking a blue or red ball is $\frac{11}{20}$ or 0.55.

(c) There are 0 black balls and 20 balls in total so the probability of picking a black ball is $\frac{0}{20}$ or 0 (it is impossible).

When working out the probability of two consecutive events, the probabilities of each individual event are multiplied together.

Example

Work out the probability of throwing a four on a normal dice and then getting a head when tossing a coin.

The probability of a four is $\frac{1}{6}$ and the probability of a head is $\frac{1}{2}$.

The probability of both events happening one after the other is $\frac{1}{6} \times \frac{1}{2} = \frac{1}{12}$.

Examiner's tip

It is sometimes useful to draw tree diagrams for questions of this type, e.g:

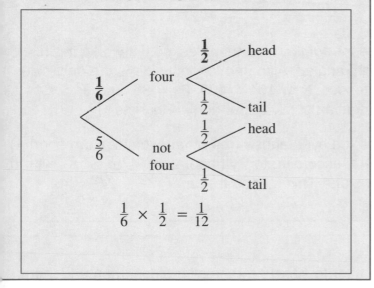

$$\frac{1}{6} \times \frac{1}{2} = \frac{1}{12}$$

Quick Questions

1 What is the probability of throwing a regular ten-sided dice and getting a score which is:
   (a) an odd number
   (b) a multiple of 3
   (c) a prime number?

2 A fairground game involves throwing a ball onto a grid. The player wins a prize if the ball falls into a lettered hole: L is a large prize, M a medium prize and S a small prize. If the ball falls in an unmarked hole the player loses.

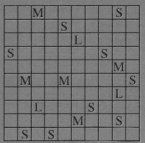

When using the game above:
   (a) what is the probability of winning a prize of any size?
   (b) If you win a prize on the game above, what is the probability that it is: (i) small (ii) medium or large?

3 On the journey to work, a motorist passes through two sets of traffic lights. The probability that she has to stop at the first set is 0.6 and the probability that she has to stop at the second is 0.4. What is the probability that on her journey to work she
   (a) does not need to stop at either set of lights (b) has to stop at the first set only (c) has to stop at one set of lights only?

What you need to know

Pythagoras' theorem or **rule**, as it is sometimes called, is about right-angled triangles.

The longest side of any right-angled triangle is opposite the right angle.
It is called the **hypotenuse**.
In any right-angled triangle:
   the square of the hypotenuse is equal to the sum of the squares on the other two sides.
This is Pythagoras in words.
(In this diagram a, b and c represent the lengths of the right-angled triangle's sides.)
Pythagoras can also be written in symbols as $a^2 = b^2 + c^2$.

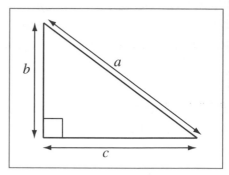

Examples

(a) Show that a triangle with sides (in centimetres) of lengths 6, 8 and 10 must be a right-angled triangle.
(b) The two short sides of a right-angled triangle are 7 cm and 24 cm long.
   What is the length of the third side?

Answers

(a) Pythagoras' theorem is only true for right-angled triangles, so if it works for this triangle, the triangle must be right-angled. Also, the longest side is the only side that could possibly be the hypotenuse. Now $10^2 = 100$, $6^2 = 36$, and $8^2 = 64$ and $36 + 64 = 100$, so the triangle must be a right-angled triangle.

(b) The side we don't know must be the hypotenuse (the other two sides are shorter), so calling the length of this side a, according to Pythagoras $a^2 = b^2 + c^2$, with b and c the lengths of the shorter sides. This means that $a^2 = 7^2 + 24^2 = 49 + 576 = 625$, so as $a^2 = 625$, then $a = \sqrt{625} = 25$.

Examiner's tip

When finding the hypotenuse remember to square the smaller sides, then add them, then take the square root of this, e.g. if $a^2 = 3^2 + 4^2$, then $a^2 = 9 + 16 = 25$, so $a = \sqrt{25} = 5$.
A very common mistake is to think, for example, that if $a^2 = 3^2 + 4^2$ then a must be $3 + 4 = 7$. This is *wrong*.

Square roots are not normally simple numbers, so you may need to round your answers.
For example, according to a calculator

$$\sqrt{20} = 4.472135955.$$

We would normally give this correct to 1 decimal place (d.p.). This is 4.5 and $4.5^2 = 20.25$, so 4.5 is a reasonable approximation.

Example

Calculate these correct to 1 decimal place:

(a) $\sqrt{203}$ **(b)** $\sqrt{5^2 + 5^2}$

(c) $\sqrt{8^2 + 4^2}$

Answers

(a) $\sqrt{203}$ to 1 d.p. is 14.2

(b) $\sqrt{(5^2 + 5^2)} = \sqrt{(25 + 25)} = \sqrt{50}$

which is 7.1 to 1 d.p. (It is NOT 5 + 5 = 10!)

(c) $\sqrt{(8^2 + 4^2)} = \sqrt{64 + 16} = \sqrt{80}$ which is 8.9 to 1 d.p.

Quick Questions

1 Here are the lengths of the three sides of some triangles. Which of them are right-angled triangles?
   (a) 17 cm, 8 cm, 0.15 m
   (b) 0.9 m, 4.1 m, 4 m
   (c) 7 cm, 5 cm, 2 cm
   (d) 99 cm, 20 cm, 1.01 m

2 The two short sides of a right-angled triangle are 255 cm and 32 cm long. What is the length of the hypotenuse?

3 Find to 1 d.p. the value of x in these expressions:
   (a) $x^2 = 200$
   (b) $x^2 = 300$
   (c) $x^2 = 6^2 + 3^2$
   (d) $x^2 = 6^2 - 3^2$
   (e) $x^2 = 16^2 - 8^2$

What you need to know

Most questions will involve you finding the right-angled triangle to use Pythagoras on. Once you have done this it should not be too hard. It usually helps to draw a sketch.

Example

1 The two sides of a square are 20 cm long.
What, to 1 d.p., is the length of its diagonal?

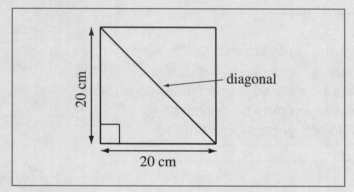

Answer

This is the situation, so by Pythagoras, the diagonal length is:

$$\sqrt{(20^2 + 20^2)}$$
$$= \sqrt{(400 + 400)}$$
$$= \sqrt{(800)}$$

which to 1 d.p. is 28.3

---

2 A large garden in a park is in the shape of a square. The distance between diagonally opposite corners is 35 m. How long is each side of the garden? Give your answer to 1 d.p.

This is a sketch of the situation.

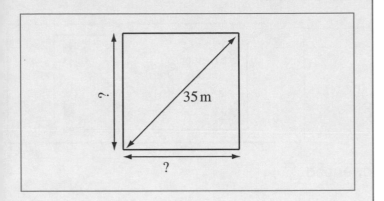

Answer

Let the sides of the square be x metres.
So using Pythagoras gives
$35^2 = x^2 + x^2$
so $2x^2 = 35^2 = 1225$
so $x^2 = 1225 \div 2 = 612.5$

which means that $x = \sqrt{612.5}$
which to 1 d.p. is 24.7 metres.

Quick Questions

4 A boat sails 20 km due south and then 12 km due west.
How far is it from the starting point?

5 A ladder is 5 m long. Its foot is on a flat driveway 2 m from the base of a vertical wall. How far up the wall will the top of the ladder reach?

6 A and B are two points on a co-ordinate grid.
A is at (1, 1) and B is at (5, 7). Calculate the distance between A and B.

7 The diagonals of a rhombus bisect each other at right angles. A rhombus has diagonals 20 cm and 14 cm long. How long are its sides to the nearest millimetre?

8 This is a sketch of the cross-section through a garden shed. Calculate the length of the sloping roof. Give your answer to the nearest centimetre.

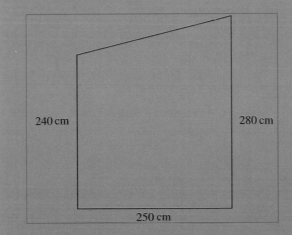

240 cm   280 cm

250 cm

This section of a garden is a lawn 6.00 metres long and 3.50 metres wide.

6.00 m

3.50 m

(a) Work out the area of this section of the garden.

The garden has triangular flower beds in each corner and a well surrounded by paving stones at the centre.
The vertical and horizontal sides of the flower beds are 1.20 metres long.

flower bed

well

(b) Work out the area of a single flower bed.

The centre of this section contains a well surrounded by six paving stones.
The radius of the outer circle is 1.00 metre.

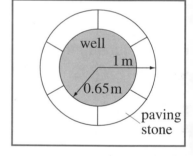

well

1 m

0.65 m

paving stone

(c) Work out the circumference of the well.

(d) What area is covered by one paving stone?

This diagram shows the side view of the well.

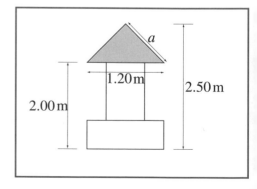

a

1.20 m

2.50 m

2.00 m

(e) Work out the length (a) of the sloping roof.

Answer

(a) Area $=$ length $\times$ width
$= 6.00 \times 3.50$
$= 21.0\,\text{m}^2$

The answer in (a) and (b) is an area the units must be 'square'.

(b) Area $= \frac{1}{2} \times 1.20 \times 1.20$

$= \frac{1}{2} \times 1.44$

$= 0.72\,\text{m}^2$

Use the correct units.

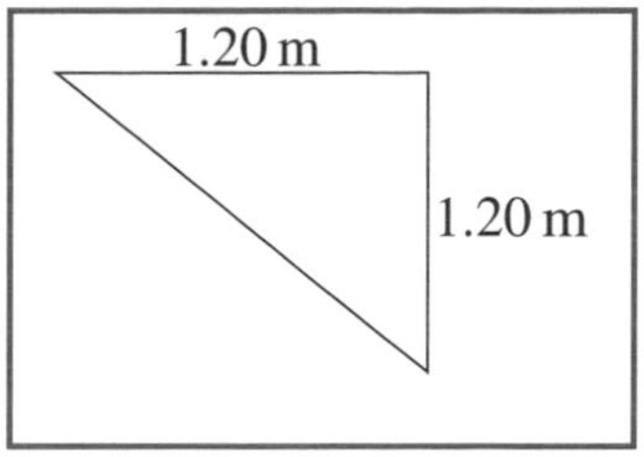

(c) Circumference $= 2 \times \pi \times r$ **You must remember the formula.**
$= 2 \times 3.142 \times 0.65\,\text{m}$
$= 4.08\,\text{m}$ **This is a distance: do not use square units.**

(d) Area of paving $=$ Large circle $-$ small circle
$= (\pi \times 1.0^2) - (\pi \times 0.65^2)$
$= 3.142 - 1.327\,\text{m}^2$
$= 1.815\,\text{m}^2$

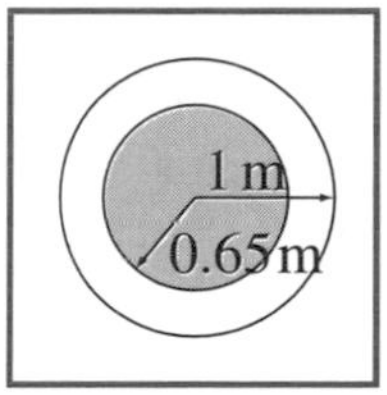

Area of 1 stone must be $\frac{1.815}{6}\,\text{m}^2$ **Make sure you answer the question asked.**

$= 0.30\,\text{m}^2$ **The area of 1 stone only is required.**

(e) Pythagoras $a^2 = b^2 + c^2$
$a^2 = 0.6^2 + 0.5^2$
$a^2 = 0.36 + 0.25$
$a^2 = 0.61$
$a = 0.78\,\text{m}$ (nearest cm)

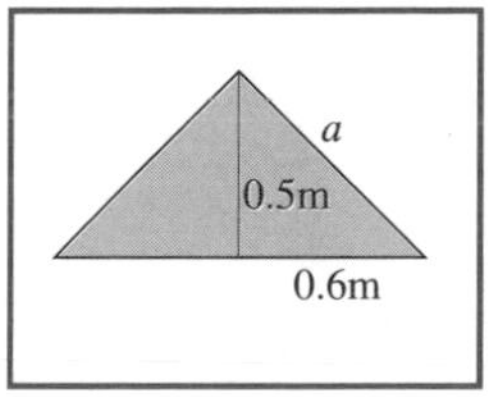

Examiner's tip

You need to use Pythagoras' rule and you must remember the formula for yourself.
Make sure you work out the dimensions of the triangle correctly from the information
in the diagram.
Give your answer to a sensible degree of accuracy.
As long as a is the hypotenuse (sloping side) it does not matter which side is *b* or *c*.

Fractions and percentages

1 (a) $\dfrac{3}{7}$ (b) $\dfrac{3}{5}$ (c) $\dfrac{3}{20}$ (d) $\dfrac{3}{4}$

2 (a) 0.222 recurring   (b) 0.125   (c) 0.857142 recurring

3 (a) 15 kg   (b) 60 kg   (c) 22.5 m

4 (a) $\dfrac{75}{170}$ or $\dfrac{15}{34}$ (b) $\dfrac{45}{170}$ or $\dfrac{9}{34}$ (c) $\dfrac{50}{170}$ or $\dfrac{5}{17}$

5 $\dfrac{8}{24}$ or $\dfrac{1}{3}$

6 (a) $\dfrac{9}{20}$ (b) $\dfrac{1}{5}$ (c) 1   (d) $\dfrac{17}{20}$

7 80%

8 First bag $\dfrac{3}{25}$ or 12%,   second bag $\dfrac{2}{20}$ or 10%. The first bag has the larger percentage of bad potatoes.

9 $\dfrac{17}{50} = 34\%$, $\dfrac{14}{40} = 35\%$, $\dfrac{9}{30} = 30\%$. Best performance is $\dfrac{14}{40}$, worst is $\dfrac{9}{30}$.

10 $\dfrac{97}{1053} \times 100 = 9.21177$ to the nearest 0.1% this is 9.2%.

11 (a) $1200 \times \dfrac{35}{100} = 420$ g (b) 780 g

12 (a) $\dfrac{86}{100} \times 125 = 107.5$ g (b) $\dfrac{5}{100} \times 125 = 6.25$ g (c) $\dfrac{7}{100} \times 125 = 8.75$ g

The rules of algebra

1 (a) 3   (b) 5   (c) 3   (d) 3

2 (a) $4x + 5y$ (b) $6x + 10y + 2z$

3 (a) $4(2 + 1) = 12$ (b) $5(6 - 1) + 5 = 30$ (c) $2(3 + 3) + 3(1 + 1) = 18$
   (d) $5(1 + 3 + 6) + 3 = 53$

4 (a) 2.94   (b) 8.18   (c) 5.66   (d) 5.76   (e) 15.95   (f) 1.61

5 (a) $6t + 6y$ or $6(t + y)$ (b) $10a$ (c) $7c$

6 (a) 10   (b) 25   (c) 50   (d) 0   (e) 10

7 (a) 64   (b) 2   (c) 24

8 (a) 32bc (b) 20xy (c) 6x + 3xy (d) 4x^2 + 8xy (e) 6x^2 + 12xy

---

Formulas and equations

1 (a) 180   (b) They should stop – maximum safe rate is 185.

2 (a) 10 metres   (b) Pat was right – maximum of 105.625 metres was reached.

3 (a) $n = 7$ (b) $c = 1.5$ (c) 8

4   5.4

5   The answer must be more than 9 because $9^2 = 81$ but less than 10 because 10^2 is 100. Liz needs to choose values between 9 and 10 and square them until she find one that gives 90. Working to 2 d.p. is enough.

6 (a) $7x - 8 = 13$ solution $x = 3$ (b) $6x + 5 = 47$ solution $x = 7$

7   The length is 125 cm and the width 100 cm.

8 (a)

(b)

(c)

(d)

9 (a) $100 < C < 200$ (b) $3 < T < 5$ (c) $18 \leq A$ or $A \geq 18$
   (d) $S > 70$

Calculations, estimates and different numbers

1 (a) 19 688   (b) 18   (c) 15

2 (a) 150 mm (b) 475 mm (c) 4750 mm   (d) 17 inches   (e) 201 inches

3 (a) $120 \times 30 = 3600$ (b) $120 \div 40 = 3$
   (c) $120 \times 1.5 = 180$ or $130 \times 1.5 = 195$

4 (a) 7 CDs: £35 ÷ £5   (b) 10 Cds: £50 ÷ £5 (actually you would only be able to
                              buy 9 as 10 would cost £49.00).

5 $350 \div 50 = 7$ cartons or $400 \div 50 = 8$ cartons are reasonable calculations

6   Jaki is wrong: the numbers generated are odd numbers some of which are not prime.

8 For example, 27, 35, 51, 57, 65, 77, 87, 93, 95.

9 (a) 4, 8 and 32 are all multiples of 2.   **(b)** 4 is one of the factors of 28 and 36.
(c) 30 and 40 are both multiples of 10. **(d)** 5 and 25 are both factors of 50.

Imperial and metric measures

1 200 g flour 50 g butter 150 ml milk

2 (a) 1350 g **(b)** 275 mm **(c)** 10.5 km(very rough), 11.2 km   **(d)** 846 litres

3 (a) metres, to the nearest metre   **(b)** grams, usually to the nearest 25 grams
(c) kilometres, to the nearest kilometre   **(d)** metres, to the nearest metre
(e) degrees, to the nearest degree

4 (b), (c) and (e)

Coordinates and graphs

1 A (0, 6) B (2, 0) C (7, 1) D (8, 7)

2

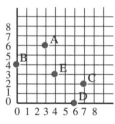

3 (a) (0, 1) (1, 3) (2, 5) (3, 7) (4, 9), etc. **(b)** (0, −2) (1, 2) (2, 6) (3, 10) (4,14), etc.
(c) (0, 2) (1, 5) (2, 8) (3, 11) (4, 14), etc   .
(d) (0, −1) (1, 1) (2, 3) (3, 5) (4, 7), etc.

4

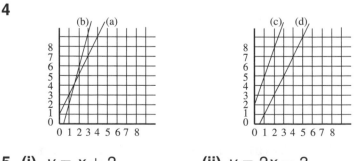

5 (i) $y = x + 2$ **(ii)** $y = 2x - 3$
(iii) $y = -x + 4$, note this is − because the line falls from left to right.

6 (a) 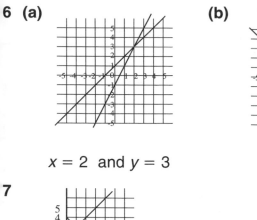 **(b)**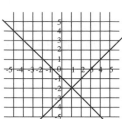

$x = 2$ and $y = 3$ $x = 1$ and $y = -2$

7

$x = 1$ and $y = 3$

Angles in polygons

1 1080°

2 146°

3 No. The angles given add up to 530° but the sum of the internal angles of a pentagon should be 540°.

4 123° each.

5 (a) 62° **(b)** 143° **(c)** 37° **(d)** 81° **(e)** 99°

6 For the external angles given, the internal angles of the triangle would be 43°, 67° and 60°. These angles add up to 170°, but the sum of the angles in a triangle are 180° and therefore the angles given must be wrong.

Angles and parallel lines

1 (a) 126° (vertically opposite angles)
 (b) 126° (corresponding angles)
 (c) 77° (vertically opposite angles)
 (d) 77° (corresponding angles or alternate angle with c)

2 (a) 73° (corresponding angles)
 (b) 49° (sum of angles in a triangle)

(c) 49° (corresponding angles)
(d) 41° (small triangle containing *c* has angles of 49°(*c*), 90° and 41°;
d is therefore equal to 41° as a vertically opposite angle)

Congruence and similarity

1 (a) A and E are congruent.
(b) B and F are similar.
A, C and E are similar.

2 (c) Not possible to tell. You need either angles A and G to be equal or sides CD and EF to be the same length. They would then be congruent.

Circles

1 (a) 254.5 cm^2 **(b)** 75.4 cm

2 (a) 45.5 cm^2 **(b)** 46 cm

3 (a) 357 metres, to the nearest metre.
(b) 6963 m^2 to the nearest square metre.

Sequences

1 (a) 25 and 28: adding on 3 each time.
(b) 81 and 100: a sequence of square numbers.
(c) 27 and 30: some multiples of 3.
(d) 26 and 42: adding the previous two terms.

2 (a) 4P + 5   **(b)** 25 − 3P

3 (a) $x^2 + 2x - 1$ **(b)** $x^2 - 2x + 4$

4 (a)

Cross Beams per side	Stays per side
1	0
2	2
3	4
4	6
5	8
.	
.	
n	$2n - 2$

(b) S = 2C − 2   **(c)** S = 4(2C − 2)

5 Roses = 4 × panels + 2

Statistics

1 Mean is 88.4 seconds; Range is 23 seconds.

2 Mean is 5; Median is 5; Mode is 0.

3 Jean: Mean 11.4; Median 11.4; Mode 11.4; Range 0.8 (11.8 − 11.0).
Sue: Mean 11.6; Median 11.8; Mode 11.8; Range 1.0 (12.0 −11.0).
From this information it can be seen that the best time of each athlete is the same.
The range of times for Jean have a smaller range and the Mode, Median and
Mean times are all lower – this means Jean is a more consistent runner.

4 Distribution A:
Number of students was 11: Mean 4; Mode 4; Range 9 (9 − 0).
Distribution B:
Number of students was 9: Mean 5; Mode 5; Range 9 (9 − 0).

5 Draw pie chart as follows: Hot 88° (24%); Salad 68° (19%); Packed lunch 79°
(22%); Snack bar 103° (29%); Go home 22° (6%).

6 (a) about 25% **(b)** about 10% **(c)** about 75%
(d) about 20%

Probability

1 (a) $\frac{1}{2}$ ($\frac{5}{10}$) or 0.5 **(b)** $\frac{3}{10}$ or 0.3 **(c)** $\frac{2}{5}$ ($\frac{4}{10}$) or 0.4

2 (a) $\frac{17}{100}$ or 0.17

(b) (i) $\frac{9}{17}$ or 0.53 **(ii)** $\frac{8}{17}$ or 0.47

If you gave answers of (i) $\frac{9}{100}$ or 0.09, (ii) $\frac{8}{100}$ or 0.08, then

you have misunderstood the question since it assumes that you win a prize and
the total number of possible outcomes is now 17 and not 100.

3 (a) 0.24 **(b)** 0.36 **(c)** 0.50

Pythagoras

1 **(a)** right-angled **(b)** right-angled **(c)** not right-angled
  (d) right-angled

2 257 cm

3 **(a)** 14.1 **(b)** 17.3 **(c)** 6.7 **(d)** 5.2 **(e)** 13.9

4 23.3 km

5 4.6 m

6 7.2 units

7 12.2 cm or 122 mm.

8 253 to the nearest centimetre.

Letts Educational
Aldine Place
London W12 8AW
Tel: 0181-740 2266
Fax: 0181-743 8451
e-mail: mail@lettsed.co.uk
website: http://www.lettsed.co.uk

First published 1999
Reprinted 1999
Text, design and illustrations: © BPP (Letts Educational) Ltd 1999

Prepared by *specialist* publishing services, Milton Keynes

British Library Cataloguing in Publication Data
A CIP record for this title is available from the British Library.

Printed in Great Britain by Ashford Colour Press

ISBN 1 85758 913 0

Letts Educational is the trading name of BPP (Letts Educational) Ltd